T0208891

Here's What You Do!

Your economic survival guide

Robert Beadles

iUniverse, Inc.
New York   Bloomington

Here's What You Do!
Your Economic Survival Guide

iUniverse books may be ordered through booksellers or by contacting:

iUniverse
1663 Liberty Drive
Bloomington, IN 47403
www.iuniverse.com
1-800-Authors (1-800-288-4677)

ISBN: 978-1-4401-3276-6 (sc)
ISBN: 978-1-4401-3277-3 (ebook)

Library of Congress Control Number: 2009903427

Printed in the United States of America
iUniverse rev. date: 4/14/2009

Contents

Preface

Let me first say that I love my country, and there is no other place in the world where a guy like me could do what I do and prosper from it. Nowhere on this planet do we have the God-given rights we have here in the United States of America. Here, you have the ability to be a success if you so choose. It is your choice. That is why so many foreigners come here year after year and do overwhelmingly better financially than those of us born right here in America.

As I have been writing this book, tonight, for the first time in the history of the United States of America, an African-American man has been elected as our president. This would have been a mere joke twenty years ago, but today our great country has become greater.

In this book, you will learn my opinion on the world and this country, along with what goes on in them. I will give you my take on the financial crisis that has been brewing, and what may come. It is not necessarily fact or fiction, but merely my beliefs and sharing how I invest and do business. I do not recommend that you do as I do unless you are mentally, emotionally, and monetarily able—and even then, although this is what I do, it may not be right for you.

I am a businessperson, investor, and landlord. I am not a writer, as you will probably soon learn. I am, however, a fairly successful young man who did not graduate college. I dropped out. I saw no reason for it. I was headed down a path that wasn't right for me. I did not want to be an employee making my bosses money, and as soon as I got enough gumption, I quit my job and went off on my own.

Although I am not super rich, if what I write about here happens, and I do believe it will, then I will be comfortably rich, being able to buy whatever my family or I need.

As I said, I am a businessman. I own construction companies in California. I have tried over the past few years to help some of my employees, ones that would accept my help, and with nothing more than their paychecks and my advice, they have gone on to become financially free, as well as homeowners. These guys don't even have high school diplomas. They're not brain surgeons, just regular people, like me, working in construction.

I am not a professor, an accredited teacher, or an author. Hell, this is the most I have typed or written in I don't even know how long. For years, I have been reading books by Robert Kiyosaki, Richard Duncan, G. Edward Griffin, Michael Maloney, and Donald Trump. I love their works, and their writings have basically molded my beliefs in their wisdom.

I have gone to countless seminars and met thousands

of financially successful people, and there always seems to be this overwhelming outcry of *What do I do?* They may be millionaires or beyond, but they believe what they know and how they obtained their wealth may soon be obsolete, like so much computer software. One day something's hot stuff; a year later, it's trash. Same, same.

So I decided to write this book after hearing the same thing time and time again: *What do I do?* I hope this answers the cries of the wealthy, middle class, and the poor. I will do my best to give a short answer for each issue, backing it up in plain English. I'll use small words with hopefully big meanings. I hate picking up books with big words and having to try to decipher their meanings. It takes too long. I'll try to get right to the point.

This book will be brief yet hit on many points. If you want more reading, you will find at the end of this book a list of what I believe are must-reads from absolutely impeccable, brilliant authors, most of whom are responsible for my education … and this book you are about to read. Throughout this book, I will throw out names and Web sites as well; I have not been paid to do so. I am simply giving you my resources, listing those places and people that have made me successful. I have them to thank, and maybe they and I can do the same for you. However, be forewarned that I am not rendering legal or accounting advice. If legal advice or other expert assistance is required, you should seek the services of a competent professional.

By picking up this book, you have taken the first step; what you do after you put it down is entirely up to you.

Introduction:

Conspiracy Theory

It is said by some conspiracy theorists that the world is controlled by just a few families. The CFR (Council on Foreign Relations) is leading us right now into a one-world government. Voting is pointless; a higher power manipulates gold and silver prices; and the future has already been planned out for us, with a predetermined fate. The same theorists say that in 1913, the richest people in the country created the Fed, via the Sixteenth and Seventeenth Amendments, to keep the rich, rich and the poor, poor, and that eventually the currency will be diluted to such a point that it has no value. They will then institute a new currency and repeat the process.

Theorists also say that the Rothschild family secretly runs this world. It is openly reported that Amsel Rothschild has said, "Give me control of the economics of a country, and I care not who makes her laws."

Forbiddenknowledge.com says that his descendants meet twice daily in London to dictate to the world what the price of gold will be, as well as what the Fed will do with America's finances. The same theorists say the Rothschilds worship Satan and that they booked a front-row seat to 9/11, watching the whole thing happen from luxury suites across the way. Under Clinton's presidency, it was said that descendents of Amsel Rothschild were wed at the White House. They also say that the Rothschilds control the money, and he who controls the money controls the governments.

Theorists say that in 1904, Rockefeller designed the public school system—the one we still use. They say it was designed to promote able-minded workers and such. That is why it lacks so horrifically in financial education. Think about it: training a bunch of future employees, not investors and business owners.

It is also said that the dollar will crash about a year and a half from now, probably in 2010, causing a global financial crisis, allowing the form of a dictator to come in, as history has consistently shown, and through population control, weed out or kill millions to instill socialism or worse. They say we should have rations and such for at least a year's worth of time—and to stay out of sight while they're trying to sort out this upcoming mess. I am not a Mormon, but I hear they have taken a lesson from the Boy Scouts in being prepared. The Mayans predicted a huge change or the end of the world in 2012. In the year 1514, Pope Leo IX said the world could end in 2014.

In the case of silver and gold manipulation, according to GATA (Gold Anti-Trust Action Committee), they have been tracking, checking, and monitoring the current and historical prices of precious metals, and they claim to have proof that the price is indeed being manipulated. It is said that if they again get their day in court, it will be fact, not a conspiracy theory anymore. Theorists also say that Elvis is alive; we were never on the moon; our government was behind 9/11; and we all came from monkeys. No matter what you believe, or how crazy this seems, I assure you that the masses will not be prepared for the things to come. You have to decide for yourself that whether fact, fiction, or what the hell, being prepared never hurt anyone.

I do not agree or disagree with any of the above. I have no proof, nor do the conspiracy theorists that make such claims. After all, a good conspiracy is one without proof; otherwise, it would be fact. You can take this with a grain of salt or heed the unknown and prepare for it.

Chapter 1

Why should I take action?

Today the country is heading toward a depression. Simultaneously, our country is looking for hope and change. And for the first time, we just elected a black man as president of our great country. If that is not change, I certainly don't know what is. However, whether you voted for McCain, Obama, Mickey Mouse, or not at all, we definitely know there is something wrong with our economy.

I truly believe that we are at a pivotal point, where something terrible is about to occur, such as a global financial meltdown, global socialism, or worse. We need to take action now to secure our financial freedom and well-being. Do not think for one moment that anyone we elect is going to make a significant difference in our bank accounts or asset columns. It took millions upon millions of dollars to earn the presidency. Where do you think Obama got the money? Teaching? Nope. Try special interest groups and whatnot. The same parties that paid the way for him to pave the way will have a price for Obama to pay for their cash contributions. Presidents care only about the bottom lines, profit margins, and moving on to the next piece of business at hand, surely not the moralities of their decisions and actions.

Hans F. Sennholz, in the book *Age of Inflation Continued*, writes, "Surely politicians have a code of laws to observe and obey, but honesty in matters of debt and money is not one of them." We the people are responsible for our own finances. The government may help in the form of welfare, tax cuts, stimulus checks, and so forth, but will those make you rich? Will a thousand-dollar stimulus check buy you the car of your dreams? Will that seven-thousand-dollar tax cut buy you the home of your dreams? Will the welfare checks feed your family what you truly want to eat? The answer? Of course not! But if those things *are* enough for you and your loved ones, simply tear out the pages of this book, place them near your toilet, and use them for toilet paper, as this book will not be for you.

I truly believe that our dollar is being printed at a point of no return. I feel the dollar will go the way of the peso. I am afraid the middle class will be wiped clean out of this country.

For years, I have told people, including my family, to get out of stocks and their 401(k)s, and to hedge their retirement in gold and silver. Unfortunately, many did not listen. They left their money in stocks and mutual funds, and have since watched all their hard-earned money simply vanish from their statements.

I was, however, able to help my father. He did listen …

somewhat. He did take all his retirement out of stocks and such, placing his money into municipal bonds. I would have preferred gold and silver, but at least his retirement money wasn't in the account when the bottom fell out on Wall Street.

To fight off inflation, I urge people to get out of low-interest-paying investment vehicles. Inflation is eating away at our dollar like Chinese termites, which eat through steel and concrete. Simply put, inflation is caused by the Fed firing up the ole printing press and pumping out more freshly printed dollars. They essentially do this every time you hear the phrases "bailout," "rescue bill," "stimulus package," and "big business low-interest loans." The more dollars they print, the less all our dollars are worth. It is just simple dilution of the money pool. This simple act is what caused the fall of Rome and thousands of other empires throughout history.

Throughout history, currencies collapse, governments fall, and yet gold and silver are always the ones to survive. The paper money never does. I truly feel this is on the way for the United States. I feel that if you and I do not stand up for our financial well-being, we will be run over like the millions before us, as has always happened throughout history. The middle class is wiped away, the rich get richer, and the poor get poorer.

The simple reason the rich get richer is that their assets, whether buildings or stores, increase tremendously in price. What I mean is that as the dollar loses value, it will take more and more dollars to buy the same things. For example, a Pepsi costs fifty cents today; tomorrow it could cost fifty dollars. Let's say you make twenty dollars an hour. If you worked eight hours, you would only be able to buy 3.2 Pepsis. See where I am going with this?

Imagine a store packed with inventory. It all goes up in price, yet the middle class and poor people's incomes stay the same, wiping them out. This may seem insane, ludicrous, or downright impossible. This however again, happens all throughout history. Check it out if you don't believe me.

Again, I will list a bunch of must-reads at the end of this book. The one that addresses this subject the most is Michael Maloney's *Guide to Investing in Gold and Silver*. His book is packed full of examples, with two hundred fact-filled pages. He takes you from the conception of money to where it has gone and where he believes it is going. He told me, though, that the editor cut out some five hundred-plus pages, feeling it contained too much information. Hopefully, he will come out with three more books to get us the rest of the info.

What I am about to say may seem, again, crazy, but history has shown this happening repeatedly. When a currency or government collapses, the people of the land are typically thinned out by force, with a dictator arising and some sort of communism or socialism taking form. Not necessarily in that order. Here are some examples: Hitler, Mussolini, Stalin, Saddam Hussein, Pablo Escobar, Shaka Zulu, Idi Amin, Omar al-Bashir, Robert Mugabe … There are hundreds, if not thousands, more. You may say, *Yeah, but this is the United States; it wouldn't happen here.* I'm sure that's what all the other countries said. As of the time of this writing, the United States has only been around for 233 years; it's just a baby in comparison to some other past empires.

Don't fool yourself: the United States is an empire. We reach across the globe, and all listen to our voice. The problem in doing this is that it overextends our wallet. When we are helping our allies, third-world countries, and so forth in funding their problems, it takes money away from our own problems here in our country. We are forced to print more money or borrow more money from other countries. Either way, we go deeper in debt. Again, every time you hear "bailout" or "stimulus package," here comes the Fed, pressing the print button, and inflation's hot on the dollar's tail. This will eventually lead to the demise of the dollar.

Ron Paul has been speaking of such for years. Unfortunately, his run for the presidency and cries for change fell upon deaf ears. The masses passed him by like a kid selling Chiclets on the streets of Mexico. This is a terrible thing. The American people and so-called delegates have no idea how badly they screwed up by not electing him. He could have made a serious change—possibly saved us from what I fear will come.

Again, this may seem crazy, and I tone my thoughts down from the next chapter on, but I believe we should keep rations on hand, just in case this mess turns out the way history shows us it can. It may seem nuts to store food, water, fuel, guns, ammunition, and so on. Truly, though, what's the harm? If I am wrong, you will have a bunch of Spam for breakfast, ammo for hunting or targets, fuel for your vehicles, and water bottles for your kids' activities. If I am right, however, you will be glad you read this book and took action.

People may call me cuckoo for my statements in this book, especially the traditional investment advisors and financial planners. That's fine; I have big shoulders, and I can carry the load. For the people who listen, though, they can judge me down the road.

For months prior to the election, I told people Obama would win. People called me crazy. *A black man?* they said. *Are you kidding?* I told them then that people were hurting and wanted change. They said, *Not that bad.* These arguments against me were coming from black, whites, and Hispanics. Guess what? He won. Now they say, of course, that people wanted change. They still wouldn't admit I was right, that they were wrong, or even offer a slap on the back, saying, *Nice call.*

Nevertheless, I called it prior to it becoming common knowledge. I know small achievement in psychic powers. But I'm not claiming to be psychic—merely a guy who knows this has happened throughout history. For all our sakes, I hope that I am full of shit and simply typing for exercise here.

Sadly, though, history says otherwise. We are at that pivotal moment, much like in 1929. The bigger problem is that now more than ever, we the people demand more help from the government. We know from history that the more help they give, the more liberties they take. When we start lining up in bread lines because we have no money to buy food, the end of our republic is near. Socialism is quickly approaching, as is what I spoke of earlier. Please read on if you think this might be possible … or you feel your financial freedom is worth protecting.

Chapter 2
What do I do?

In a simple sentence, buy gold, silver, and real estate ... and apply for money! Take whatever money you can afford to spend—that which does not affect your groceries, rent, mortgage, etcetera—and buy gold or silver. You can buy much more silver than gold and much more gold than real estate. So buy in relation to the status of your cash on hand. In the following chapters, I will get into my reasoning behind buying gold, silver, and real estate.

If you cut back on unnecessary spending—such as eating out, video game and movie purchases, emotional shopping, late night eBaying, and so forth—and put that money toward, say, the purchase of silver, you will soon see what greater good it will do for you.

I truly believe that our dollar is about to die in value. I believe the Fed is printing money like it's going out of style, and whomever holds on to the dollar will find out the hard way, as has every civilization, that fiat money returns to zero in value sooner or later. *Fiat* means backed by only the word, promise, or good faith that the government is good for it. The dollar used to be backed by gold. But in 1971, President Nixon took the dollar off the gold standard. It is now called fiat currency.

Don't think for a second that the Brits or anyone else is safe either. They backed their currency by our dollar, and once our dollar was no longer backed by gold, everyone else's currency became fiat at the same time. I will go into more detail later in the book.

In your spare time, get hold of the National Grants Foundation, where you will find grant writers and much more. Give them a call, telling them your story, and your dreams, aspirations, and goals, and see if they can recommend a government program that may fit your situation. The government offers free money in the form of grants; they also offer loans and subsidies if you are a fit for one of these programs they are trying to fund, help, or get started.

Example: A working mom in Michigan wants to quit her job and spend more time with her kids, but she can't afford it. Maybe she applies for a grant to become a babysitter in her neighborhood, getting the money she needs to set up shop and pay the bills while she gets started. The government can give her money for it! Why not take advantage of your tax dollars?

Example: A roofer in New York wants to start his own business. He gets his roofing license and then applies for a small business loan or subsidy. The government cuts him a check for the materials, equipment, etcetera to get started, or gives what is called a subsidy, where the equipment is purchased for him.

Again, call the National Grants Foundation; they will write your business plan and help you every step of the way. If you cannot afford the writing fees, you can write it yourself with their help. They will walk you through every step of the way. Imagine getting a million bucks for six thousand dollars in fees. It seems well worth it to me. But every situation is different. It may not be right for you. I will discuss grants more in a later chapter.

Chapter 3
Why gold and silver?

As I stated in chapter 1, the dollar was backed by gold prior to 1971, when President Nixon took us off the gold standard. In doing so, he simultaneously turned the world's money into fiat currency. Countries across the globe backed their currency to ours. For example, the British pound was backed by U.S. dollars, which were backed by gold. By taking the United Sates off the gold standard, the Fed and the U.S. Treasury are now able to print as much money as they want, backed by nothing more than a promise that they arc good for it.

Picture this: There are two dollars in existence; you have a dollar in your hand, and the bank has a dollar in its hand. Out of thin air, the Fed prints two more dollars and gives them to the Treasury, which gives them to the bank. Your dollar has just lost 50 percent of its purchasing power! The unfunny thing is that this constantly happens, on a smaller scale, every month.

If you can, think back to when the median home price was forty thousand dollars; now it's over two hundred thousand. A dinner that cost five dollars is now twenty-five. The value of the home or meal did not go up over all these years, but the price did. How does this happen? It's called inflation. Every time they print more money, there is more money chasing your money, diluting it and causing it to become worthless, as every currency has always become. Thousands of times throughout history, currency backed by nothing eventually becomes worth nothing. This is fact! No fiat currency has ever survived. Don't be fooled into thinking ours will.

Ours has failed twice before: there was the continental in 1775 and the greenback in 1862. They failed for many reasons, but mostly due to overprinting the money, causing rapid inflation—similar to what is happening today. There have been talks of our new currency being called the Amero. It would be a joint currency of Mexico, America, and Canada. Will it happen? Who knows? I do know this: the dollar is on life support right now; it has a terminal illness and will be dead soon enough. What replaces it, we can only speculate.

Gold and silver, on the other hand, have always been around and have always been used as currency. They don't need backup or buddies. They have worth on their own and always will. They will always be able to purchase goods and services when your dollars will not.

Gold and silver once there price is to be known you will probably see seven thousand dollars for an ounce of gold and five hundred for an ounce silver … they could go much, much higher before the dollar dies. If you are savvy, once gold and silver prices rise, you will go buy as much real estate as possible, or pay off your existing mortgages. The market will have to readjust, a new currency will come about, and you will own a bunch of real estate that you can rent or sell out at the new currency price!

This may sound scary or absurd to some, but I assure you, this has happened numerous times throughout history. It will happen again. Look at Rome. It was in power for centuries, but once it started doing as we are, printing money from nothing, it burned and collapsed, even with a strong army. A country cannot survive without a strong, stable currency.

Look at Iceland. The country has gone bankrupt and is being parted out and bought up at pennies on the dollar. Small comparison, I know, but still plausible. We will soon be following, as our mortgage-backed securities were responsible for crippling their economy.

In summary, gold and silver have always maintained value and always will. Even in 1933, when Roosevelt made it illegal for U.S. citizens to own gold, it was $20 per ounce. When President Ford, in 1973, legalized gold once again, it opened at $35 per ounce. That is a 57 percent gain. It may not seem like a lot of money in 1973, but it hit over $200 in 1974, going up another 1000 percent. Remember, that was back before our crazy printing spree. Money actually had worth back then ... to some extent. As I write this book, gold has previously hit $1000 an ounce. It is currently at $730 an ounce. Silver was at $3 back then, has been to $35, and is currently at $10. Once the lid blows off this Cracker Jack box, the sky's the limit!

You might be thinking, *This all sounds good, but where*

do I go? Where can I buy these supposed miracle metals? Doing so is actually quite simple and discreet. You can buy gold and silver from local coin and jewelry stores, pawnshops, and so forth. However, I recommend buying online and having it sent to either a secure vault, such as the one offered by Brinks, or mailed right to your door so you can bury it out back if you so desire. (Where you put it is your choice—but it should be somewhere out of the reach of would-be thieves.)

I also recommend buying bullion only. What this means is basically non-numismatic coins and bars. The American eagle one-ounce coin is a great place to start in silver. You can move up to ten, fifty, one hundred, or even one thousand-plus one-ounce bars if you so desire.

Again, I would not, nor do I buy collector coins or jewelry. Collectable coins and such are referred to in the industry as numismatic. The chance of getting ripped off is much greater as they are charging you for a supposed collectable value atop the current spot price—*spot price* meaning the actual asking price per ounce of silver or gold.

Here is a list of a few places where I purchase my gold and silver:

Goldsilver.com, which is owned and operated by Michael Maloney; Monex.com; Bulliondirect.com; APMEX.com; and last but not least, good ole eBay. I buy from eBay when I am hard up and no one else seems to have any silver or gold. It happens from time to time that there is simply nothing for sale, but rest assured that eBay has your back. They are a bit more expensive than your traditional choices, but when gold and silver do what I think they are going to do, who cares about buying for a couple bucks over spot?

Buying gold is much like buying silver, except for the cost. It is much higher. You simply get less metal for your buck. A single one-ounce gold coin today costs around $730; with silver just under $10, you could get seventy-three one-ounce coins. When the dollar crashes and you need to buy groceries, it will be much easier with silver, as it is worth less and will not require as much change.

At the same time, do the math: If gold reaches $7,000 and silver reaches $500, the gains will be much higher in purchasing silver today. You can get seventy-three one-ounce silver coins for $730, which is a total gain of $427 per ounce times seventy-three coins, equaling a total profit of $31,171, versus $6,270 for gold. If you initially spent $730 and gold reached $7,000 per ounce, the difference equals $6,270. Do you see where I am going here? I much prefer silver. It takes up much more space, but you can see that paying for storage shows a higher potential for profit.

There are also exchange-traded funds, or ETFs: paper, silver, and gold. Their ticker symbols are GLD and SLV; I do not buy these. Investopedia.com defines ETFs as "a security that tracks an index, a commodity or a basket of assets like an index fund, but trades like a stock on an exchange." ETFs experience price changes throughout the day as they are bought and sold. Investopedia.com says this means the following: "By owning an ETF, you get the diversification of an index fund as well as the ability to sell short, buy on margin and purchase as little as one share. Another advantage is that the expense ratios for most ETFs are lower than those of the average mutual fund. When buying and selling ETFs, you have to pay the same commission to your broker that you'd pay on any regular order. One of the most widely known ETFs is called the Spider (SPDR), which tracks the S&P 500 index and trades under the symbol SPY."

If that interests you, great—at least that's one of us. I'm sure there is a lot of money to be made buying such things, but I was always taught that if you don't understand something, don't do it or get rid of it.

That leads me to our next investment vehicle for gold and silver. Known as *futures,* Investopedia.com defines these as "a financial contract obligating the buyer to purchase an asset (or the seller to sell an asset), such as a physical commodity or a financial instrument, at a predetermined future date and price." Futures contracts detail the quality and quantity of the underlying asset; they are standardized to facilitate trading on a futures exchange. Some futures contracts may call for physical delivery of the asset, while others are settled in cash. The futures markets are characterized by the ability to use very high leverage relative to stock markets. Futures can be used either to hedge or to speculate on the price movement of the underlying asset. For example, a producer of corn could use futures to lock in a certain price and reduce risk (hedge). On the other hand, anybody could speculate on the price movement of corn by going long or short using futures.

Investopedia.com says the above definition means this: "The primary difference between options and futures is that options give the holder the *right* to buy or sell the underlying asset at expiration, while the holder of a futures contract is *obligated* to fulfill the terms of his/her contract. In real life, the actual delivery rate of the underlying goods specified in futures contracts is very low. This is a result of the fact that the hedging or speculating benefits of the contracts can be had largely without actually holding the contract until expiry and delivering the good(s).

For example, if you were long in a futures contract, you could go short the same type of contract to offset your position. This serves to exit your position; much like selling a stock in the equity markets would close a trade."

Again, I'm sure there is a lot of money to be made buying and doing such things, but again, it's not for me.

My main reason for buying gold and silver that you can touch, feel, deposit, store, or bury is simply that if the dollar or government crashes, the first thing they always default on is the paper assets. As I have stated, you can place your metals in a facility such as Brinks offers; you can place them in your local bank's safety deposit box, which I don't recommend; you can place them in your home safe, in your basement, under your bed, in your backyard, etcetera—wherever you are most comfortable. But wherever you keep them, make sure you can get to them in case of emergency. That's why I don't recommend your local banks. Most are closed on weekends, nights, and holidays, and they can also find out what you have in your deposit box.

As Robert T. Kiyosaki has stated, "Savers are losers." I believe what he means is that if you just keep putting your cash in the bank or 401(k)s, you might get wiped out. Invest in your future. No one else will. Don't leave your future to chance.

If you think leaving your money in the bank or retirement accounts is safe, think again. If inflation doesn't eat your money like locusts, and the dollar keeps from crashing, you will still be no better off tomorrow than you are today. Why stand idly by and watch your money evaporate before your eyes or, at best, just stay the same?

As I said earlier, the median price of a home was around forty thousand dollars; now it's over two hundred thousand. The value didn't go up; the price did. That was totally due to inflation! It has happened all too often throughout history. Don't think for a second that we will be luckier than those before us. History tends to repeat itself.

Personally, I am hedging my bets. I know gold and silver will always be of value. The dollar will not. But before you run out and empty all your accounts to buy gold and silver, remember that you still have bills to pay and obligations to keep in the meantime. This is merely what I do; this may not be right for you: I buy the following one-ounce gold coins: South African Krugerrands, Gold Mexican Pesos (these guys range in ounces), Canadian Maples, Chinese Pandas, Gold Buffalo Coins, and American Gold Eagles. I will give you Monex.com definitions of the Krugerrand and American Gold Eagle. I prefer these, as they are heavily traded and well known.

The Krugerrand as defined by Monex.com:

> While there are a number of gold coins available on the market, the South African Krugerrand is the original one troy ounce gold bullion coin made by a government and valued on the content of its gold, rather than the face value of the coin. Originally minted in 1967 in an effort to help market South African gold to the international market, the Krugerrand stood alone as an accessible

investment opportunity for the everyday buyer ... it was the first gold coin to contain exactly one troy ounce of gold, and was intended from its inception to provide a way for the private investor to purchase precious metals. The Krugerrand derives its name from combining the names of Paul Kruger, a well-known Boer leader and local hero who went on to become the last president of the Republic of South Africa, and the "rand"—the monetary unit of South Africa.

The obverse side of the coin is detailed with a profiled bust of President Paul Kruger and features the name of the country, "South Africa," in the country's two native languages, English and Afrikaans. The reverse side of the coin features the image of a springbok antelope, one of the national symbols of South Africa, originally used on the South African 5-shilling piece. The reverse side also features the year of issue and the fineness of the coin.

The South African Krugerrand is a 22-karat coin weighing a total 1.0909 ounces (or 33.930 grams). It is comprised of one troy ounce of pure gold and 2.826 grams of a copper alloy which is used to give the coins higher durability and to make them more resistant to scratching, and gives the coins a unique orange-gold hue.

The gold Krugerrand has a diameter of 32.6mm, a thickness of 2.74mm, and has a fineness of .9167, or 22 karats.

**Here is how Monex.com describes the
American Gold Eagle:**

> Coins produced in America, the original $10
> gold "Eagle" coins, were originally minted by the
> United States Mint starting in 1795. More than
> two hundred years later, U.S. gold coins—perhaps
> some of the greatest symbols of American liberty
> and freedom—are still produced with levels of
> quality and beauty that one would expect of the
> United States Mint.
>
> First released by the United States mint [*sic*] in
> 1986, the gold American eagle [*sic*] is the first
> modern bullion coin to be authorized by the
> United States congress [*sic*] ... and is backed by the
> US [*sic*] Mint for its weight, content and purity.
>
> Each gold American eagle [*sic*] coin features
> striking imagery, symbolizing the American spirit
> and character. The obverse of the coin, originally
> designed by Augustus Saint-Gaudens for the
> country's $20 gold piece minted from 1907 to
> 1933, carries the image of a full[-]length figure
> of Lady Liberty holding a torch in her right hand
> and an olive branch in her left. In the background
> can be seen the images of the sun rising and the
> United States Capitol dome. The obverse side of
> the coin also bears the inscription "Liberty" and
> contains both the date of issue and the individual
> mint mark of origin. The reverse side of the coin
> bears the image of a male bald eagle carrying an
> olive branch, flying towards his mate in a nest with
> their hatchlings.

The one-ounce gold American Eagle has a diameter of 32.7mm, a thickness of 2.87mm, a total weight of 1.0909 troy ounces (or 33.931 grams), contains one troy ounce of pure gold, and has a face value of $50. One-ounce gold American Eagles are sold in units of 10 one-ounce coins.

Each of the fractional gold American Eagle coins [is] sold in units of 20 coins each. The half-ounce gold coin has a diameter of 27mm, a thickness of 2.15mm, a total weight of .5454 troy ounces (or 16.966 grams), contains a half ounce of pure gold, and has a face value of $25. The quarter-ounce gold coin has a diameter of 22mm, a thickness of 1.78mm, a total weight of .2727 troy ounces (or 8.483 grams), contains a quarter-ounce of pure gold, and has a face value of $10. The tenth-ounce gold coin has a diameter of 16.5mm, a thickness of 1.26mm, a total weight of 0.1091 troy ounces (3.393 grams), contains a tenth-ounce of pure gold[,] and has a face value of $5.

Like the South African Krugerrand, all American Eagle gold bullion coins are 22[-] karat (or .9167 fine) gold, containing an alloy of silver and copper to help increase the stability and scratch-resistance of the coins. Each coin is guaranteed to contain an exact quantity of gold, mined exclusively in the United States, and to meet the rigid quality standards of the U.S. Mint.

American Eagle gold coins provide investors with the means to diversify, balance and stabilize a well-rounded investment portfolio, all with the safety and backing of the United States government and the U.S. Dollar.

I thought this information above would be useful so you can see some technical data behind the coins; the above comes from one of the most respected gold and silver dealers in the world. I used their exact words from their Web site, as they are the experts and know the intricacies of the coins they sell.

G. Edward Griffin, the author of *The Creature of Jekyll Island*, said that if a ship carrying our dollars sank in the ocean today, no one would dive down to retrieve the cash a hundred years from now. But if it were gold or silver, it would be a different story. What I think he is saying is that cash is trash. Why risk your life for it? It will be worth nothing in a hundred years. Think about it: it hasn't even been in existence for a hundred years and look how bad off it is. Before it, the greenback and continental came to rise and fall terribly—just as our current dollar is doing now.

I believe the best way to save yourself is by purchasing gold and silver. These metals fight off inflation and don't lose value. They may go up and down in price, depending on who is manipulating them. But I assure you this: their value has always been the same, though their price has not. Their prices will shoot like a star; I'm just not sure when. People smarter than I say a year and a half, and others as smart as they are say maybe four or six. Who knows? But this I do know: get ready. Do all you can now, for tomorrow may be too late.

Chapter 4

Why real estate?

Throughout time, people have always needed housing. We have always needed a roof over our heads … and always will. Be you a homeowner, house flipper, single-family landlord, multifamily landlord, or a commercial building landlord, you will always be needed.

It is said that 90 percent of all millionaires and above have acquired their fortunes primarily through real estate. This is not a new concept; it has been around for thousands of years. If you read the previous chapters, you will see that I base all investments on gold and silver—and what they will buy me. I also try to purchase as much real estate as I can now, using today's currency, putting as little down as possible, in hopes that tomorrow's gold and silver price will go up astronomically, allowing me to pay off the debt on the mortgages with a little gold and silver, owning the property outright. Is this foolproof? No. Anything can happen, but as history has always shown, it does in fact happen. Which side will you be on: profiting from cheap money, or losing everything because of the cheap money?

Example: In Mexico, the peso was at a seven-to-one ratio with the dollar in the 1980s. The government made the dollar illegal to own and required the citizens to turn over their dollars for seven pesos. The citizens did, as they could no longer pay for goods with the dollar. The next day, the government devalued the peso to a ratio of seventy to one against the dollar.

Do you see what has happened? The middle class was obliterated. The businesspeople, store owners, landlords now had property and merchandise worth tenfold more than the day before, able to charge the new rates as well. The poor and middle class, however, could not afford the new prices, causing a huge transfer of wealth, and depression took place. The same will likely happen here in the United States.

When Roosevelt made gold illegal in 1933, he defaulted on all paper backed by gold—stealing approximately 40 percent of the U.S. currency supply. He robbed us blind, but had he not, the United States would have failed and gone belly-up back then. If the people's assets had been in gold, silver, or real estate—especially the latter—they would not have been as affected by Roosevelt's paper theft.

If you think you cannot afford an investment of property or a home, think again. All day long, I see single-family homes that start at ten thousand dollars! Look in places like Tulsa, Oklahoma; they are out there.

Can you not ask family or friends for a two-thousand-dollar loan or increments that can help with a down payment, sell stuff on eBay, cut back on BS spending, put it on your credit cards?

Look at it this way: Your mortgage would be somewhere around a hundred bucks a month. You could easily rent the house out on Section 8 for seven hundred a month. You would make an additional six hundred per month before this huge transfer of wealth hits, and then make a huge profit when you pay it off with your gold or silver and sell it or rent it out at the new currency rate.

If you are wondering what Section 8 is, it is a government program done throughout the United States, in which it pays you, as the landlord, a set amount each month to put one of its qualified families in your property. They typically pay for the first, last, and monthly rents. I believe they even pay for repairs if their families damage your property. Each county has its own program; for information, call the housing authority phone line.

Another great thing about real estate is your tax benefits. You can write off so much money! It is a beautiful thing when you can make money every month off positive cash flow and depreciate the property at tax time, getting a fat tax check just for making your mortgage payments!

Let me give you an example of one of the deals I have done. I purchased a home in Stockton, California, for $40,000, and I remodeled it for $30,000. I had a total of $72,000 in the project. I listed the property with the government under their Section 8 program. The Section 8 inspector came out, saw that the home was fit for a family to live in, and approved the home. I then picked the tenant and made another agreement with the tenant to pay an additional $155 per month, as this was now a remodeled home, not some slum house, as some Section 8 homes are.

The Section 8 sends me $795; the tenant gives me $155. That is a total of $950 per month … $11,400 per year. This is essentially 15 percent on my money each year. That's nothing, though, because I just had the house appraised in today's market—at $149,000. I also receive nice tax deductions in the form of depreciation, and if there was a mortgage on the property, I could write off all the interest. I could, in theory, refinance the house and be in it with zero money out of pocket (suck out my original $72,000 investment, creating a $72,000 mortgage), still collecting several hundred dollars in profit each month, even with a mortgage!

However, I have not done so at this time. I will just keep it the way it is for now. It is rather nice owning homes free and clear. It's refreshing to get all that cash flow every month, making money in my sleep. Money coming in minus expenses leaves you with extra money called cash flow.

Some people call me crazy. They say I should refinance and buy more, and there is definitely some serious validity to their opinions. If it were an apartment complex, without a doubt, I would refinance the property. It would definitely make me more money every month and allow more transactions with the money. However, refinancing single-family properties can be tricky; it may provide cash flow wonderfully today, but after refinancing, it may become upside down tomorrow.

There is only one rent collected for a single-family home; you are somewhat handicapped in how far you can raise the rents. You are somewhat handicapped in price as well. You may have the nicest home on the block, but if the other houses are crap, they will bring down the price of your house.

Apartments are different. Banks look at how the property cash flows; that is how they determine a price for each unit or the whole complex. You have much more opportunity to make greater amounts of money once you go commercial, above four units.

Back to the example of the property I purchased. I know you are probably saying that you don't have $72,000 lying around, so how can you afford it—where can you get the money? Look, you are only limited by your own mind. Homes start at $10,000. Buy one, putting down 20 percent out of pocket; Section 8 it; collect the cash flow; and repeat. It truly is that simple.

If you are looking for places to invest, I suggest going to www.ofheo.gov, which is the Office of Federal Housing Enterprise Oversight. Check out the quarterly reports labeled the "House Price Index." This little gem is packed full of useful information that shows where the prices of homes are going up, down, flat, and much, much more.

I also love Huduser.org; this little beauty shows fair market rents for all areas in the United States. Think how useful this could be once you locate an area using ofheo .com; then you can see what the rents are for your chosen area. These will give you a fairly educated guess on where to buy and what you can expect to get for rents.

If you notice, I don't act much like a house flipper. That's because I'm not. I am in it to win it! Flipping houses can be lucrative. I'm not saying it's not, but historically it's not. If you kept the properties, you would see over time, through cash flow and appreciation, that it stomps flippers.

Flippers are in it for short-term gains. It's possible, but if you look at all the flippers of the world today, you will see that most have gone the way of the dodo. However, there are exceptions. Richard Davis of Trade Mark Properties is an absolute expert at flipping, and he has done extremely well for himself and others. Armando Montelongo is entertaining and obviously very successful at flipping properties.

So, obviously, it can be done, and to contradict myself, there might even be an appropriate time. Example: You purchase a property for, say, one hundred thousand dollars. Before you close on the deal, someone offers you two hundred thousand for it. That's a no-brainer. Say you buy a chunk of land, subdivide it, and sell 50 percent of the parcels, which pays off the original mortgage; you keep the other 50 percent of the parcels, build homes on the parcels, and sell the homes. Is this flipping? Yes … and, again, it can be done, but if you are not a Mr. Davis or Mr. Montelongo, you could be in a world of hurt if something goes bust.

I recommend stupid simple: buy a house, rent it out, collect the cash flow, and repeat. It is a surefire way to accumulate a tremendous amount of wealth safely. It won't happen overnight, but if you follow the recipe, you will become wealthy.

Look at 2001–2005. Did you see the huge transfer of wealth? Did you see how real estate went up drastically in price? I believe it was due to a crashing stock market and the Fed throwing around cheap money.

In 2001, the financial advisors, planners, investors, bankers, and others transferred monies from a failing stock market into mortgage-backed securities, causing a tremendous boom in house prices.

But we all know about booms; they have busts. If you played your cards right, you may have bought prior to 2001 and sold in 2004, and are now buying again in 2009. If not, I suggest you take another look. Deals are out there. It is certainly a buyer's market, and there are handsome gains and instant equity to be made.

I love the United States. What a great country we live in! What side will you be on? Profit or not?

Chapter 5

Why grants and loans?

Plainly put, why not? Why not try to get free money? Why not try to get back some of the money you have been paying out all these years? Why not apply for a loan? If something above will help you obtain greater wealth or good, why not do it? No money, you say? Guess what? There are ways to do it for nearly free. No experience in it, you say? Guess what? There are people and organizations that will do it for you, for a fee. Don't know what to use the money for? Do some soul searching; what is it you like to do? How can what you like to do become a business? How can it make you money? What if you already have a business and just want to expand? Guess what? There is money for that. If you want to go back to school or get into school, there's money out there for you. Sick of your job and want a new career? There's money for that too. No matter what your situation, you could probably find a place or a thing to throw money at. Why does it have to be your money you are throwing around? Remember, you are only limited by your mind.

Okay, let's dig in a bit. The government gives out money all the time, even to our enemies. Why can't they send some your way? The government gives us money to get something in return. To get money from them, the simplest way is to figure out what they currently need or are in the market for.

For instance, say you are currently a small business owner. Say the government is looking for a company or companies to put Latino or American Indian workers to work. By meeting there requirements, they will give you money to seek out, train, employ, and cover all kinds of expenses, including expansions and whatnot, just to fill a certain need they may have.

Say you want to buy houses but have no money. The government will give you money or a loan if you are able to fill another need they may have, such as low-income rental housing. They will throw money at you to fill their need. Same thing goes for low-income neighborhoods that lack sufficient rental properties. They may give you money or a loan to build, buy, or remodel an apartment complex.

Perhaps you want to start a business. Say you love kids, the outdoors, and sports. You may be able to get money to start some sort of sports center. You know the ones: with batting cages, football fields, basketball courts, gymnasiums. They may give you the money to start one if they have a problem with youth violence in a certain neighborhood and want some kind of program to encourage kids to stay out of trouble. Any way you slice it, there's plenty of pie to go around.

As I said earlier, they won't run out of money. They just print more. As the ole saying goes, *How can I be broke? I still have checks left.* Trust me, the government knows all about writing checks. Why not get yours?

For more information on grants, loans, and subsidies, I strongly encourage you to go to NationalGrants.com. They know their stuff. They can help design and write your grant application and business plans.

If you are like me and already have a full plate, that's great. They will basically do everything for you. You tell them what you want to do, and they will do what they can to make it happen. It really is pain free. Right now, I have them submitting business plans and applications for me on behalf of a couple of construction companies I own. The rates are extremely fair and reasonable for what your possibilities can be.

For instance, for one of my companies I own, I applied for a little expansion grant. They are trying to get 1.5 million dollars for another office location in the Bay Area to employ people the government wants working. The entire cost, whether I get the grant or not, is six thousand dollars. Not bad. They do all the legwork, all the writing, and help with the submitting and correspondence. I sit back, continue with all my other stuff, and wait for the good news. More free money. Isn't it cool?

Give it a try; what do you have to lose? Oh, and in case you don't have the six grand or whatever it may be, you can use their half-now, half-later plan. Borrow from friends or family ... or simply do the work yourself.

Either way, you will most certainly be better off than where you are today.

Chapter 6
Should we dread the Fed?

Hell, yes, we should! The Fed is called the bank of last resort. They control the country. They have essentially caused the mess we are in right now. They have allowed trillions of dollars to be bought up by Asian countries. If the Asian countries ever decide to dump these dollars, rather than to hold them, the dollar will crash overnight.

Again, every time you hear the terms bailout, rescue plan, stimulus package, or big business low-interest loan, they're firing up the ole printing presses, printing that money like they have it. Every time they print more money, ours is eaten away by the hidden tax known as inflation. Some call it the stealth tax.

Again, for example, a soda pop used to cost five cents, and now it's fifty cents. That is essentially forty-five cents of inflation tax. See where I am going here? Inflation is brutal; it is the main cause of boom and bust cycles.

Here is some more crazy inflation: The government keeps giving automakers more and more money that we don't have. It has to come from somewhere. So we either print it or borrow it as usual. This is just plain stupid. It's as though the Fed is in a race with someone to see who can dilute our currency the fastest. It is quite evident that the economy is in the tank and people aren't buying new vehicles. So why, then, should we throw money to failing, unwanted businesses?

Jobs, you say? Think of the millions who stand to lose their jobs if the automakers go under, you say? I'm sorry, but if my business were failing and I showed my balance sheet and profit and loss statements to the banks and said, "Look, I'm going to run out of cash by the end of the year if you don't throw me a big fat bone." They would call security and have me thrown out for smoking crack.

Banks don't loan to companies that don't show a profit or potential for it. The economy is in the tank, and they are currently in business. So what difference will it make if the Fed throws the automakers a couple hundred billion? None, I say. There is no evidence that in a couple of years, the economy will be as it was a couple of years ago. The money is simply delaying the inevitable. If they don't go bankrupt now, they will in a few years. Why not let it happen now? They could file Chapter 11 and, under new ownership, restructure and build vehicles much more cost efficiently.

Think about it. Even if the Fed throws them money and says, "Look, this money is for fuel-efficient vehicle development and research," it still won't help. We already have the technology for fuel-efficient vehicles. We can power our vehicles through nuclear power (the sun), using solar and electric technology. According to Peter Meisen of Geni.org, we can power the entire planet with two hundred square miles of solar panels. That's all it would take. The entire world would have free energy. But due to big oil companies, this will not happen.

So when the Fed throws money at the big three in claims of research and development, we know it's bullshit. The technology is already there—but it will not be implemented.

For shits and giggles, look at the Tesla Roadster. The technology is there; they just don't want us to have it. Look at the $850 billion they already passed. What good has it done? Fat cats got fatter. CEOs got fat severance packages, not the shareholders, citizens, or employees.

Now they are going to pass an additional $780 (plus) billion dollar stimulus bill. That's a trillion and half dollars. I hear that if you stack hundred dollar bills flat, not on their sides, but flat, one trillion dollars would reach 670 miles into space from Earth. That is going to seriously dilute our money supply. The sickest part is that most of the money goes right back to the government. It goes to building more federal buildings, more money for state agencies, cars for government employees, and so on. It is pushing socialism upon us at a much faster pace than I foresaw. The Fed and U.S. government would like to nationalize banks here shortly. That should be truly terrifying. You know, getting loans from someone broker than you. Socialism does not work. It never has and never will. This money they are playing with is not going to the people that need it. What good has all the money that has already changed hands done for the millions that are in foreclosure or the millions that lost their jobs? Nothing or very little, that's how much. Soon they will be able to print even more multitudes of money.

The Fed started this mess, and they are the ones to fix it? Come on. The lowering of interest points, the lack of oversight when they were supervising others. What happens when there are just government banks? Who is going to oversee them? What will happen to our dollar then? When they make more mistakes, they will just print more money. When someone else needs a bailout, they will just print more money. When will it all end? Well that's what this book is about. The end of the dollar.

I will be truly surprised if any substantial amount, or any, goes toward buying up the banks' bad loans—like mortgage-backed securities. I think they will probably throw a little money toward credit card companies to show some effort toward doing something to free up some lending money. Most likely, they will end up using the money to buy interest in banks so they can later absolve the bad debt and print more multitudes of money, knowing or unknowingly to us, kicking off the end of the dollar.

Here is how investorwords.com defines the Federal Reserve System:

> The central banking system of the U.S., comprised of the Federal Reserve Board, the 12 Federal Reserve Banks, and the national and state member banks. Its primary purpose is to regulate the flow of money and credit in the country. The Federal Reserve was established in 1913 to maintain a sound and stable banking system throughout the United States

and to promote a strong economy. The Board of Governors is made up of 7 members that are appointed to 14-year terms by the President and approved by the Senate. Almost all U.S. banks are a part of the Federal Reserve System, which requires that those banks maintain a certain percentage of their assets deposited with the regional Federal Reserve Bank. These "reserve requirements" are set by the Board of Governors and by changing the requirements, the Federal Reserve System can greatly impact the amount of money supply in the economy. The Federal Reserve System has several functions. First, it serves as a bank for banks: many transactions between banks are processed through the Federal Reserve System. Financial institutions are also able to borrow money through the Federal Reserve, but only after attempting to find credit elsewhere; the Federal Reserve System provides credit only when it cannot be found in the markets or in cases of emergency. Second, the Federal Reserve System acts as the government's bank. The tax system processes incoming and outgoing payments through a Federal Reserve checking account. The Federal Reserve also buys and sells government securities. The Fed even issues the U.S. currency, although the actual production of the currency is handled elsewhere. Third, the Federal Reserve System acts as a regulatory agency. The Fed polices the banking industry to make sure that things run smoothly and that the rights of consumers are protected.

Money.howstuffworks.com describes the Fed as:

> One of the more mysterious areas of the economy is the role of the Fed. Formally known as the **Federal Reserve**, the Fed is the gatekeeper of the U.S. economy. It is the central bank of the United States—it is the bank of banks and the bank of the U.S. government. The Fed regulates financial institutions, manages the nation's money and influences the economy. By raising and lowering interest rates, creating money[,] and using a few other tricks, the Fed can either stimulate or slow down the economy. This manipulation helps maintain low inflation, high employment rates, and manufacturing output.

Let me now briefly describe to you what the Fed is, in my opinion. After reading the definition from Wikipedia and How Stuff Works, it would appear that the Fed is a government institution; it, of course, is not. *What is this?* you say. Please read on.

The Fed is a private corporation in which I believe the banking business J.P. Morgan owns controlling interest. The Fed is responsible for printing money. It supplies the Treasury with cash. It is immune to external oversight and audits. It has the power to control our economy. In simple terms, the way our money system works is this:

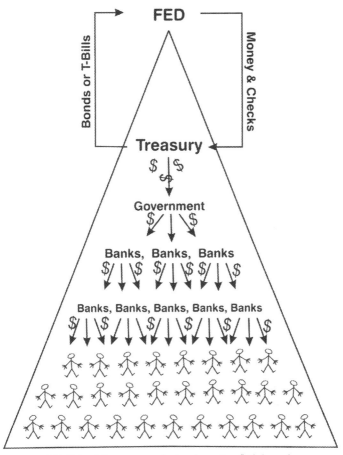

All this Money printed out of thin air.
See the problem?

The Treasury sells T-bills or bonds to the Fed; the Fed prints the money and sends it to the Treasury. The Treasury sends the money to commercial banks; the commercial banks send money to smaller banks; and smaller banks send us cash in forms of loans. However, along each step of the way, the money sent is kept and sent out in what is called fractional reserve banking.

Simply put, say I get one hundred dollars from the bank and loan ninety dollars to you; you can loan eighty dollars to Bob; Bob can loan seventy dollars to Bill; and so on.

But do you see where this all has gone horribly wrong? In the beginning, the Fed wrote the check to the Treasury; and the Treasury wrote the banks a check, which wrote me a check; then I wrote you a check, while the initial money that came from the Fed came from thin air! It didn't come from the Fed's vault; they simply printed more money.

The dollar, by design, is meant to crash and lose value. The country's richest people designed the Fed in 1913 on Jekyll Island. It was designed for themselves, not for you or me. You cannot beat them. So why not join them? Without this system, the country would never have been able to expand and build as it has through using debt and loans. If you can understand how to leverage money profitably for yourself through real estate and other investments, their system will benefit you.

I believe Bucky Fuller once said, "If you can't make money, at least make sense." He was referring to socialism, I believe, and if people don't get into the game soon, it is where we will be heading.

Every time the masses cry out for financial help from the government, the government takes more of our freedoms, and eventually this will result in socialism. Someone once said, "War unites us; peace divides us." Look at 9/11. Afterward, there was an overwhelming outcry for help, protection, and vengeance. It gave birth to the Patriot Act.

Have you ever read it? It's some scary shit if they ever apply all of it or even some of it. What's next?

The Fed is not unique to the United States alone; all central banks and countries do the same. They just go by different names. There are higher powers at work here; they know what they are doing. When this currency crashes, where will you be, leveraged to the gills in real estate loans, sitting on gold and silver? Or stuck with your head in the sand saying, *Please not me*?

The old saying that you can lead a horse to water, but you can't make him drink applies here. Think small if that's what it takes; instead of buying that Blu-ray DVD, buy three ounces of silver and so on. You can thank me later. The main point I really want to drive home is simply this: every dollar was literally created from thin air. There was nothing backing it.

The Fed has supplied the United States with funny money. Every time the Fed prints more money they charge the U.S interest on that funny money. Every dollar ever created has been borrowed into existence. There is no way the U.S. government could ever pay back the money. It was all borrowed, even if they paid back the principal, they would never be able to pay off the interest. They would have to print more money and then again, pay interest on that money. It is definitely a confusing system. That is the way it was designed to be.

There is no changing it; you can only use it. Without this system, our country would be much smaller and much less developed. We wouldn't have all the retail stores, hotels, airports, amusement parks, diners, movie theaters, grocery stores, gas stations, and whatnot without this system. In my opinion, it was designed to eventually dilute the money supply into extinction. You need to figure out where this puts you. Victim or victor?

Use the system to your benefit and possibly reap the rewards, or hang around doing nothing, getting nothing, hoping nothing happens. But we all know where nothing leads. It is as Joe Biden calls Sarah Palin: bridge to nowhere. So get off your ass and take charge. Be that person your family counts on to provide for them. Aspire to be more, do more, have more. In this great country, you can. All you have to do is take action. Start small, miss small. Some action is better than no action. Do something even if it's wrong. Just make sure it's legal.

Chapter 7
Here's what you do! Let's recap:

Okay, let's go back over this stuff one last time:

- The dollar is about to be completely diluted. Get rid of it. Don't hang on.

- Buy gold and silver.

- Buy real estate.

- Apply for grants, loans, and subsidies.

- Get into debt! Make the payments. Pay it all off once the currency dies and gold and silver make their move!

- Have a year's worth of rations of food, water, fuel, guns, and ammo, just in case. Better safe than sorry.

Chapter 8
Suggested Reading

I hope this book has been useful to you. I hope you have gained some insight and have decided to take action to obtain your own wealth. I cannot take action for you. I truly believe a storm is coming, and without arming yourself with financial education and the will and desire to change, you will certainly be sunk. I strongly recommend you read the following books, as I have the utmost respect for these guys. In addition to their books, they have been personally inspiring and enlightening to me, and have also served as resources for this book.

- *Rich Dad, Poor Dad*, Robert T. Kiyosaki (the guy is brilliant)
- *Rich Dad's Prophecy*, Robert T. Kiyosaki
- *Rich Dad's Guide to Investing*, Robert T. Kiyosaki

- *Rich Dad's Increase Your Financial IQ*, Robert T. Kiyosaki
- *The ABC's of Real Estate Investing*, Ken McElroy
- *The Advanced Guide to Real Estate Investing*, Ken McElroy
- *The Creature from Jekyll Island*, G. Edward Griffin
- *Guide to Investing in Gold and Silver*, Michael Maloney (the guy is a genius)
- *The Dollar Crisis*, Richard Duncan
- *How to Build a Fortune*, Donald Trump
- *Why We Want You to Be Rich*, Robert T. Kiyosaki & Donald Trump
- *Real Estate Wealth System*, James Smith

1) I also recommend all of the *Rich Dad* series books by Robert Kiyosaki, Blair Singer, Ken McElroy, Michael Maloney, and other Rich Dad's Advisors. They have spent years trying to educate others financially when their methods and opinions were not publicly popular. Now, more and more, it is just becoming common sense and fact. They have been speaking for years on what is happening now, and what is to come. They are all good reads so dive in while you still can.

2) Another author you might want to check out is Ann Coulter. She packs quite the punch. I believe she has five best-selling books and is not afraid to talk about the issues.

3) Alex Jones is another great writer and filmmaker. He's not like Michael Moore. He actually gets to the truth or tells it, rather. He doesn't leave out the important stuff. If you think I'm doom

and gloom when it comes to what's going on and what's coming you need to check him out. He's on the radio, at Infowars.com and Prisonplanet .com. Do not miss out on watching his movie *Endgame*. It will surely open your eyes. You can buy it at Prisonplanet.com; it's well worth the twenty bucks.

4) For political straight talk when you're out and about you should give a listen to either Alex Jones, Michael Savage of *Savage Nation,* or for a more mild-mannered approach but still good, try Sean Hannity.

Resources

Web Sites

Investopedia.com

Goldsilver.com

RichDad.com

Gata.org

Theforbiddenknowledge.com

Monex.com

Ofheo.gov

Huduser.org

En.wikipedia.org

Money.howstuffworks.com

Nationalgrants.com

Google.com

SBA.gov

Firstgov.gov

GSA.gov

Hud.gov

Fedstats.gov

CNN.com

Investorwords.com

Books

Rich Dad, Poor Dad, Robert T. Kiyosaki

Rich Dad's Prophecy, Robert T. Kiyosaki

Rich Dad's Guide to Investing, Robert T. Kiyosaki

Rich Dad's Increase Your Financial IQ, Robert T. Kiyosaki

The ABC's of Real Estate Investing, Ken McElroy

The Advanced Guide to Real Estate Investing, Ken McElroy

The Creature from Jekyll Island, G. Edward Griffin

Guide to Investing in Gold and Silver, Michael Maloney

The Complete Idiot's Guide to 2012, Synthia & Colin Andrews

Freakonomics, Steven D. Levitt & Stephen J. Dubner

Age of Inflation Continued, Hans F. Sennholz

About the Author

Robert Beadles is currently thirty-one years of age and married to a beautiful woman, with two handsome boys. He was wed at the young age of seventeen, prior to his first son's arrival. He was poor and struggled tremendously to make ends meet. He is the son of a loving and supporting yet financially middle-class father and mother. He worked hard, taking on several jobs to support his new family.

He graduated high school in 1995 by means of an adult high school diploma. Robert went to college and majored in administration of justice, with potential hopes of becoming a police officer. He dropped out, as he was drawn in another direction. In 2004, he read the book *Rich Dad, Poor Dad* by Robert T. Kiyosaki. It changed his life for the better. He then quit his job and started his first company.

His first company had a host of problems, as he regretfully took on a partner of no worth or value—simply a financial leech. He scrapped the company quickly when he saw where the ship was headed, creating another company with only his wife and himself as officers and owners. They haven't looked back since. Since 2005, they have created several businesses that employ hundreds of people throughout California. They have built homes, companies, investments, and strong ties in their communities. They invest in real estate all throughout the United States. They have financially educated as many as have asked and listened.

Robert enjoys time with the family, making money, martial arts, hunting, target shooting, long vacations, riding dirt bikes, reading, weight lifting, and fine dining. Robert is like a steamroller: he has just gotten going. His enormous wealth and drive have just started, and by no means does he plan to stop. He has just begun. Stay tuned.